THE HISTORY OF THE MIAMI DOLPHINS

THE HISTORY OF THE

MIAMI

Published by Creative Education

123 South Broad Street

Mankato, Minnesota 56001

Creative Education is an imprint of The Creative Company.

DESIGN AND PRODUCTION BY **EVANSDAY DESIGN**

LIBRARY OF CONGRESS CATALOGING-IN-PUBLICATION DATA

Schmalzbauer, Adam.

The history of the Miami Dolphins / by Adam Schmalzbauer.

p. cm. — (NFL today)

Summary: Traces the history of the team from its

beginnings through 2003.

ISBN 1-58341-302-2

1. Miami Dolphins (Football team)—History—Juvenile literature.

[1. Miami Dolphins (Football team)—History. 2. Football—History.]

I. Title. II. Series.

GV956.M47S26 2004

796.332'64'09759381—dc22   2003065225

First edition

9 8 7 6 5 4 3 2 1

COVER PHOTO: running back Ricky Williams

PHOTOGRAPHS BY

AP/Wide World Photos, Corbis (Bettmann, UPI/Corbis-Bettmann), Getty Images, Icon Sports Media Inc., SportsChrome USA

DOLPHINS

BOASTING YEAR-ROUND SUNSHINE AND SOME OF THE WORLD'S BEST BEACHES, MIAMI, FLORIDA, IS A PICTURE-PERFECT PARADISE. IN THE 1920S, THE CITY EXPERIENCED A POPULATION EXPLOSION AS AMERICANS FROM THE NORTH FLOCKED SOUTHWARD. IN THE 1960S, MANY CUBANS IMMIGRATED TO MIAMI AS WELL, GIVING IT A LARGE SPANISH-AMERICAN POPULATION. THE MIAMI METROPOLITAN AREA IS TODAY HOME TO ALMOST THREE MILLION PEOPLE AND IS VISITED EVERY YEAR BY MORE THAN 10 MILLION TOURISTS. IN 1965, ANOTHER NORTHERNER—A MINNESOTA LAWYER NAMED JOE ROBBIE—BROUGHT PROFESSIONAL FOOTBALL TO MIAMI IN THE FORM OF A NEW AMERICAN FOOTBALL LEAGUE (AFL) FRANCHISE. WHEN IT CAME TO CHOOSING THE TEAM'S NAME, ROBBIE AND TEAM OFFICIALS CONSIDERED SUCH POSSIBILITIES AS THE MARAUDERS, MARINERS, SHARKS, AND SUNS. IN THE END, THOUGH, THE TEAM WAS NAMED THE DOLPHINS AFTER ONE OF THE FASTEST AND SMARTEST CREATURES OF THE SEA.

[1972 Miami Dolphins]

DOLPHINS FANS SAW some exciting performances early on, but the team struggled to win games. Speedy receiver Joe Auer returned the opening kickoff of the 1966 season 95 yards for a touchdown, and offensive tackle Norm Evans established himself as one of the AFL's best players. Still, the Dolphins would go just 15–39–2 over their first four seasons.

Things began to change for the better in 1967, when the last-place Dolphins drafted Bob Griese, a talented quarterback from Purdue University. Griese, who wore glasses, was called by some the "thinking man's quarterback." With his great intelligence and instincts, strong arm, and poise under pressure, he quickly emerged as the leader of the Dolphins.

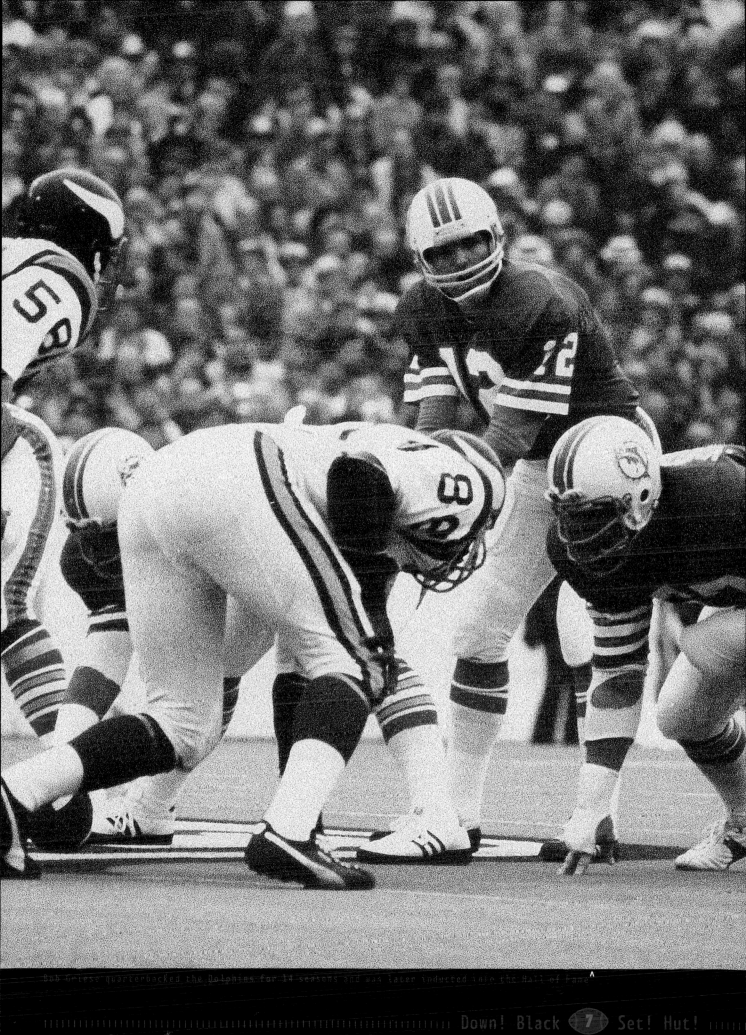

Bob Griese quarterbacked the Dolphins for 14 seasons and was later inducted into the Hall of Fame.

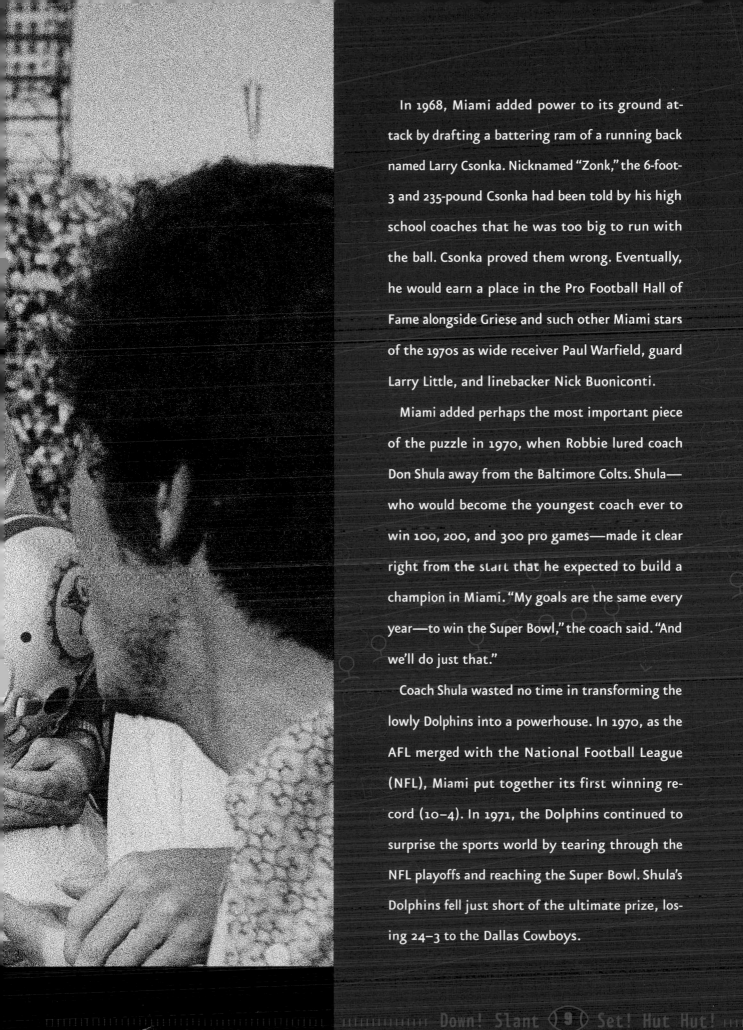

In 1968, Miami added power to its ground attack by drafting a battering ram of a running back named Larry Csonka. Nicknamed "Zonk," the 6-foot-3 and 235-pound Csonka had been told by his high school coaches that he was too big to run with the ball. Csonka proved them wrong. Eventually, he would earn a place in the Pro Football Hall of Fame alongside Griese and such other Miami stars of the 1970s as wide receiver Paul Warfield, guard Larry Little, and linebacker Nick Buoniconti.

Miami added perhaps the most important piece of the puzzle in 1970, when Robbie lured coach Don Shula away from the Baltimore Colts. Shula—who would become the youngest coach ever to win 100, 200, and 300 pro games—made it clear right from the start that he expected to build a champion in Miami. "My goals are the same every year—to win the Super Bowl," the coach said. "And we'll do just that."

Coach Shula wasted no time in transforming the lowly Dolphins into a powerhouse. In 1970, as the AFL merged with the National Football League (NFL), Miami put together its first winning record (10–4). In 1971, the Dolphins continued to surprise the sports world by tearing through the NFL playoffs and reaching the Super Bowl. Shula's Dolphins fell just short of the ultimate prize, losing 24–3 to the Dallas Cowboys.

COACH SHULA NEVER really asked his players for perfection, but in 1972, that's exactly what the Dolphins were. When Griese broke his ankle in the fifth game of the season, 38-year-old backup quarterback Earl Morrall stepped in to lead the offense. Csonka and fellow running back Mercury Morris, meanwhile, each rushed for more than 1,000 yards—a pro football first for two teammates in the same season.

The Dolphins' defense was just as impressive. Nicknamed the "No-Name Defense" on account of its shortage of star-caliber players, the Miami defense allowed the fewest points of any NFL team in 1972. "The nickname doesn't bother us," said safety Jake Scott. "I don't care if people remember my name as long as we don't have any losses."

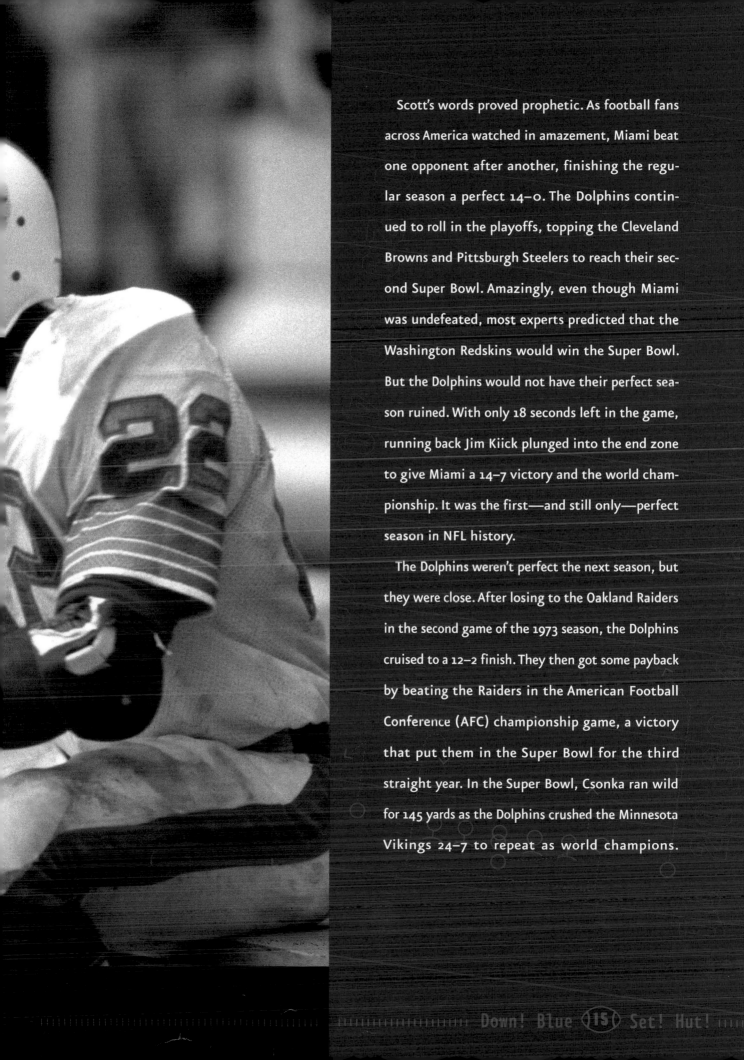

Scott's words proved prophetic. As football fans across America watched in amazement, Miami beat one opponent after another, finishing the regular season a perfect 14–0. The Dolphins continued to roll in the playoffs, topping the Cleveland Browns and Pittsburgh Steelers to reach their second Super Bowl. Amazingly, even though Miami was undefeated, most experts predicted that the Washington Redskins would win the Super Bowl. But the Dolphins would not have their perfect season ruined. With only 18 seconds left in the game, running back Jim Kiick plunged into the end zone to give Miami a 14–7 victory and the world championship. It was the first—and still only—perfect season in NFL history.

The Dolphins weren't perfect the next season, but they were close. After losing to the Oakland Raiders in the second game of the 1973 season, the Dolphins cruised to a 12–2 finish. They then got some payback by beating the Raiders in the American Football Conference (AFC) championship game, a victory that put them in the Super Bowl for the third straight year. In the Super Bowl, Csonka ran wild for 145 yards as the Dolphins crushed the Minnesota Vikings 24–7 to repeat as world champions.

MIAMI WON THE AFC Eastern Division title in 1974 with an 11–3 record. There would be no Super Bowl appearance this time, though. The Raiders proved that they were now an AFC heavyweight by beating the Dolphins 28–26 in the first round of the playoffs. The Dolphins then said good-bye to three of their brightest stars as Csonka, Kiick, and Paul Warfield left town.

Although Miami continued to post winning records in the seasons that followed, it would be another four years before the Dolphins returned to the playoffs. Still, Miami's impressive air attack—featuring Griese and new star receiver Nat Moore—kept the Dolphins exciting. In 1979, Larry Csonka returned to the team to frustrate opponents with his sledgehammer running style for one

Pro Bowl kicker Garo Yepremian made many big field goals for the Dolphins throughout the 1960s.

playoff loss, what a decade it had been. Over the course of the '70s, Miami had put together a combined 104–39–1 record and brought two Super Bowl trophies to southern Florida.

By 1980, Csonka had retired, and Griese was starting to show his age. New leaders began to step forward to keep the Dolphins flying high. One of these leaders was center Dwight Stephenson, a former All-American at the University of Alabama selected in the 1980 NFL Draft. Hailed by Alabama coaching legend Paul "Bear" Bryant as "the best center I ever coached," Stephenson would be considered the NFL's premier center within a few seasons.

In 1981, Stephenson and nose tackle Bob Baumhower led Miami to an 11–4–1 record and the playoffs. It took an overtime field goal by the San Diego Chargers in a thrilling 41–38 game to end the Dolphins' season. Then, in 1982, Miami earned its fourth Super Bowl appearance. Unfortunately for Dolphins fans, the team remained stuck on two world championships as the Washington Redskins won that game 27–17.

CALLED THE "Year of the Quarterback," 1983 saw six great quarterbacks selected in the first round of the NFL Draft. Although each of these players would leave lasting effects on their respective teams, none would have the immediate impact of Pittsburgh University's Dan Marino, chosen by the Dolphins with the 27th overall pick.

"Dan the Man," as he became known to fans, was an NFL star by the end of his first season, leading the AFC in passing and becoming the first rookie ever to start in the Pro Bowl. "You could tell right away that Danny had this unbelievable talent to throw the ball," said Dolphins receiver Nat Moore. "He was so accurate...[and] had so much zip on the ball. For me, playing with Danny was more than anything like watching an artist at work. He

Marino picked defenses apart at an even greater rate in 1984. By the ninth game of the season, he had already broken Bob Griese's team record for passing yards in a season. With the help of Miami's sure-handed "Marks Brothers"—the terrific receiving tandem of Mark Duper and Mark Clayton—Marino finished the year having set new NFL records for passing yards (5,084), pass completions (362), and touchdown passes (48).

With the help of the "Killer B's" defense (so-named because nine players' names began with the letter "B"), the 1984 Dolphins surged to a 14–2 record. While defensive linemen Doug Betters and Charles Bowser kept the pressure on opposing quarterbacks, the Dolphins offense overwhelmed the Seattle Seahawks and Pittsburgh Steelers in the playoffs to put Miami in its fifth Super Bowl. Marino predicted victory over the San Francisco 49ers in the big game, but the 49ers stunned the Dolphins 38–16.

The Dolphins reached the AFC championship game in 1985, but a 31–14 loss to the New England Patriots signaled the start of a late 1980s slide. Despite Marino's heroics, the booming kicks of punter Reggie Roby, and the tough play of young linebacker John Offerdahl, the Dolphins failed to make the playoffs again in the '80s.

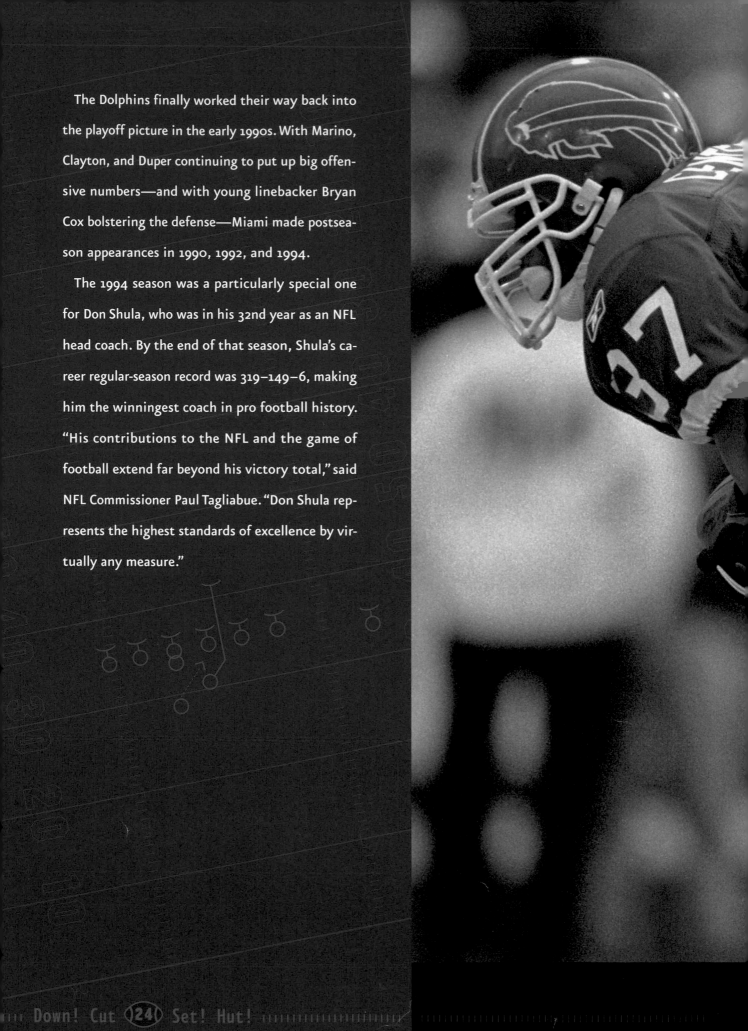

The Dolphins finally worked their way back into the playoff picture in the early 1990s. With Marino, Clayton, and Duper continuing to put up big offensive numbers—and with young linebacker Bryan Cox bolstering the defense—Miami made postseason appearances in 1990, 1992, and 1994.

The 1994 season was a particularly special one for Don Shula, who was in his 32nd year as an NFL head coach. By the end of that season, Shula's career regular-season record was 319–149–6, making him the winningest coach in pro football history. "His contributions to the NFL and the game of football extend far beyond his victory total," said NFL Commissioner Paul Tagliabue. "Don Shula represents the highest standards of excellence by virtually any measure."

SHULA WALKED THE Miami sidelines only one more season. After the Dolphins went 9–7 in 1995, he stepped down as head coach and was replaced by Jimmy Johnson. An energetic coach who had led the Dallas Cowboys to two Super Bowl victories in the early '90s, Johnson made clear right away that losing would not be accepted. "I expect results," he said, "and as long as I get results, I'll be a very happy person."

The Dolphins slowly improved under Coach Johnson in the late '90s. Miami assembled a young, attacking defense that featured linebacker Zach Thomas, end Jason Taylor, and cornerback Sam Madison. Offensively, the club was led by the aging but still effective Marino, who now slung the ball to speedy receiver O.J. McDuffie. In 1998, the year Marino became the first NFL quarterback ever to throw 400 career touchdown passes, the

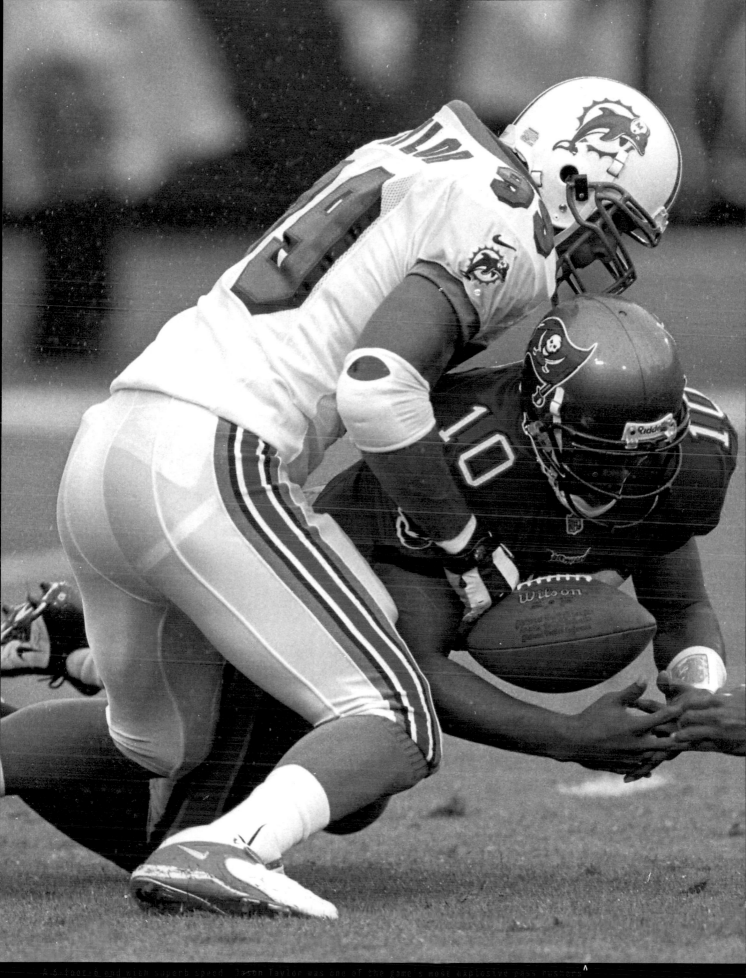

Despite his many NFL passing records, "Dan the Man" still lacked what he wanted most—a Super Bowl ring. It looked like he might get that ring in 1999 as Miami started out 7–1 and made the playoffs. The Dolphins beat the Seattle Seahawks 20–17 in round one, but their season came to a jarring end the next week with a 62–7 loss to the Jacksonville Jaguars. Just days after the humiliating defeat, Coach Johnson resigned and was replaced by former Chicago Bears head coach Dave Wannstedt. Soon after that, Marino decided to hang up his cleats, bringing his amazing 17-season career to an end.

Coach Wannstedt began rebuilding the Dolphins offense by signing quarterback Jay Fiedler. Then, in 2002, the team made the deal Dolphins fans had been waiting for since the retirement of Larry Csonka—it traded with the New Orleans Saints for star running back Ricky Williams. The 5-foot-10 and 225-pound Williams had great strength, speed, and vision, and he put them all on display immediately. The Dolphins' single-season rushing record of 1,258 yards had stood for 25 years before Williams shredded it with an NFL-best 1,853 yards in his first season wearing Miami aqua and orange. "We've had big guys and fast guys, but not the whole combination," said Dolphins running backs coach Joel Collier. "Ricky's not a talk-

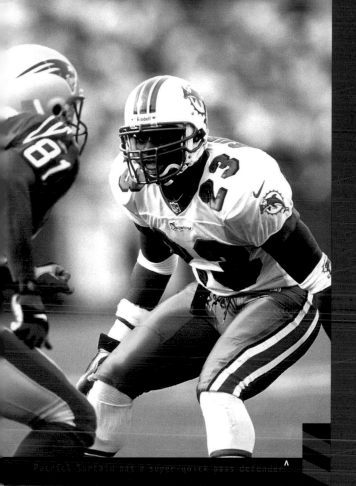

Patrick Surtain was a super-quick pass defender

Jay Fiedler was known as an intelligent leader

ative guy, but his actions make things kind of fun around here."

As Williams continued to trample opposing defenses, the Dolphins improved to 10–6 in 2003. Although the team fell just short of the playoffs, the football forecast in Miami was a sunny one. With offensive stars such as Williams and receivers Chris Chambers and David Boston, and defensive standouts such as Taylor, Thomas, and cornerback Patrick Surtain, the Dolphins were expected to make waves in the AFC East in 2004 and beyond.

In less than four decades, the Miami Dolphins have written one of the most impressive stories in NFL history—a story that includes five Super Bowl appearances, two world championships, and pro football's only perfect season. And with an all-time roster that includes such names as Griese, Csonka, Marino, and Williams, Miami fans have always found reasons to believe that their beloved Dolphins will soon swim to championship glory once more.

INDEX >